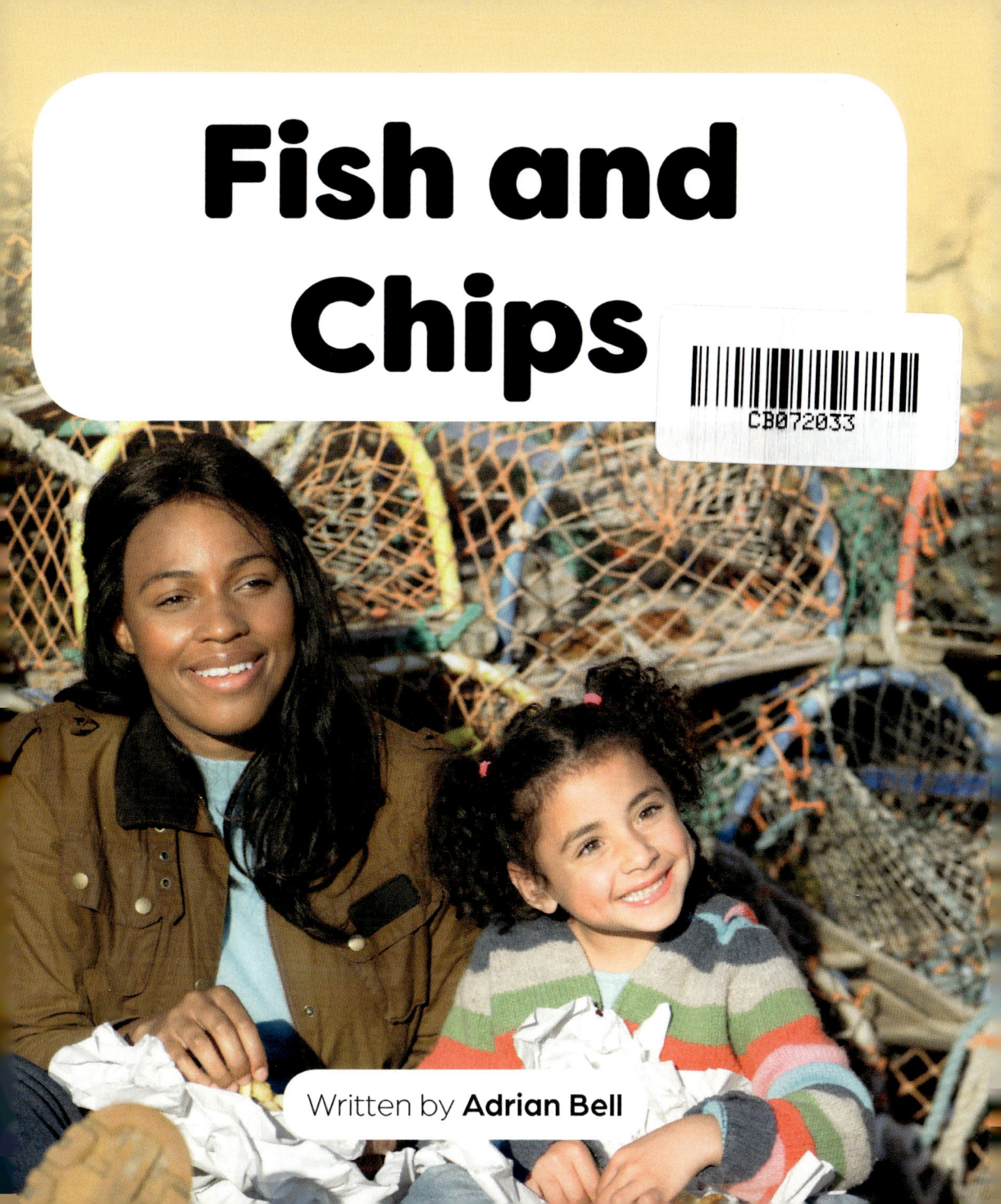

Fish and Chips

Written by **Adrian Bell**

Fast phonics

Before reading this book, ask the student to practise saying the sounds (phonemes) and reading the new words used in the book. Try to make it as speedy and as fun as possible.

Read the tricky high frequency words

The student can't sound out these words at the moment, but they need to know them because they are commonly used.

she   **we**   **the**

to   **he**   **for**   **of**

Tip: Encourage the student to sound out any sounds they know in these words, and you can provide them with the irregular or tricky part.

Say the sounds

ch   **tch**   **sh**   **ll**   **w**

The 'ch' and 'tch' graphemes can make the same sound ('ch' as in chin, 'tch' as in match). Talk to the student about this similarity and point it out in words as you come across the graphemes in this book.

Tip: Remember to say the pure sounds. For example, 'sssss' and 'nnnnn'. If you need a reminder, watch the *Snappy Sounds* videos.

Snappy words

Point at a word randomly and have the student read the word. The student will need to sound out the word and blend the sounds to read the word. For example: 'fff–rrr–e–shhh, fresh'.

fish	chips	fetch
fresh	check	patch
brush	chop	catch
chill	batch	munch
shop	children	

Quick vocabulary check

The underlined words may not be familiar to the student. Check their understanding before you start to read the book.

Mum and Dad run a fish and chip shop.

Can children help?

Yes, we can!

Children can help to dig up the plants for the hot chips.

He can fetch the spuds from the patch.

She can check and brush the spuds.

Children can help to get fresh fish.

She can get her rod and catch the fish.

Children can help in the shop, too.

She can chill the fish.

Dad can chop a batch of chips.

Mum and Dad sell the fish and chips in the shop.

We get the cash.

We munch on
the fish and chips!

Comprehension questions

Well done!

Let's talk about the story together

Ask the student:
- What did the children do in the beginning of the story?
- Why did the girl go on the boat?
- Find a word that means to keep something cold (chill).
- Do you think lots of people like to eat fish and chips? Why?

Snappy words

Ask the student to read these words as quickly as they can.

| brush | fresh | catch | batch |
| chill | cash | munch | children |

Fluency

Can the student read the story again and improve on the last time?

Have fun!